Thank You
for caring so

Friend

Thank You

much about me.

One of my fondest memories is

_____

_____

_____

_____

_____

_____

_____

_____

Thanks so much
for making our

lives anything but boring.

You showed me how much attitude matters when

_____

_____

_____

_____

_____

_____

_____

_____

Thank You
for making your

sense of humor contagious.

You have a knack for knowing when I need a lift

_____

_____

_____

_____

_____

_____

_____

Thanks for
always being truthful

...when it comes to fashion.

I found this to be true when

_____

_____

_____

_____

_____

_____

_____

_____

Thank You
for showing

me your world.

We are two separate people and your world has enriched mine by

_____

_____

_____

_____

_____

_____

_____

_____

my friend.

Your friendship was especially appreciated when

_____ ,

_____

_____

_____

_____

_____

_____

_____

Thanks so much
for inviting me

ut when I truly needed it.

I really felt rescued the time that you

_____

_____

_____

_____

_____

_____

_____

Thank You
for accepting

me for just the way I am.

It was a boost of confidence when you said

_____

_____

_____

_____

_____

_____

_____

_____

Thank You
for your gutsy

way of having fun.

You're not going to believe this but

_____

_____

_____

_____

_____

_____

_____

_____

We've been through
times when our friendship

was on shaky ground.

Thanks for sticking by me when

_____

_____

_____

_____

_____

_____

_____

_____

Thank You for making

surprises special.

Y͘ou totally surprised me when

_____

_____

_____

_____

_____

_____

_____

_____

Thanks for all
of the incredible

memories that you've given me.

Here is one of my favorites

_____

_____

_____

_____

_____

_____

_____

Thanks for the
hours of shopping...

our excuse just to get together.

If not for you I never would have found that perfect

_____

_____

_____

_____

_____

_____

_____

_____

We've listened

with our hearts,

creating a deep friendship.

One of my fondest memories is

_____

_____

_____

_____

_____

_____

_____

a necessary priority.

Remember the great time we had when

_____

_____

_____

_____

_____

_____

_____

Thanks for all
of the possibilities

that you've helped me to create.

Without your support I never would have tried

_____

_____

_____

_____

_____

_____

_____

_____

There are so many
reasons that I love you.

Thank you for all of them.

Here are just a few of my favorites

_____

_____

_____

_____

_____

_____

_____

_____

We have other
friends, but the friendship

we share is something special.

Thanks for being such an original friend. Remember when we

_____

_____

_____

_____

_____

_____

_____

_____

We love to get away from it all. Thanks for

being my partner in crime.

So many wonderful memories of mischief. My favorite is

_____

_____

_____

_____

_____

_____

_____

_____

Thank You
for blooming

and growing with me.

A few years ago no one would have believed that we would
have changed in these ways

_____

_____

_____

_____

_____

_____

_____

_____

We've shared wonderful secrets at

all times of the day and night.

Thank you for trusting me with a secret like this

_____

_____

_____

_____

_____

_____

_____

_____

Thank You

for your zany

sense of humor.

I laugh when I recall

_____

_____

_____

_____

_____

_____

_____

_____

I can always rely on you to know when

to just kick back and relax.

Sometimes I just needed to unwind and you always
had the time and place to

_____

_____

_____

_____

_____

_____

_____

_____

Thank You
for being spontaneous

when I had a quirky idea.

I just needed to laugh and have fun with you when

_____

_____

_____

_____

_____

_____

_____

_____

Thanks
for the best moments

in our friendship.

Your friendship has meant so much to me because

_____

_____

_____

_____

_____

_____

_____

_____

Thanks
for your positive attitude

that made each day brighter.

One particular time that your outlook helped me was

_____

_____

_____

_____

_____

_____

_____

_____

Our friendship has given me tremendous

comfort. Thank you.

Thanks for your support when I

_____

_____

_____

_____

_____

_____

_____

_____

When I'm
with you, fun is

always around the corner.

I think back on all the great times and I especially love this one

_____

_____

_____

_____

_____

_____

_____

Thank You
for being

a part of my everyday life.

Thanks for being there at a moment's notice when

_____

_____

_____

_____

_____

_____

_____

I am grateful for the quiet times

we shared together.

I found this to be very comforting

_____

_____

_____

_____

_____

_____

_____

Life is magnificent
with a friend like you.

Thank you.

We'll grow older, but our times together will never be forgotten.

_____

_____

_____

_____

_____

_____

_____

_____

© 2004 Havoc Publishing
San Diego, California
U.S.A.

Text by Maureen Webster

ISBN 0-7416-1310-7

www.havocpub.com

Made in Korea